One Minute Pocket Prayers

Lady A'Besa Hodge

Copyright © 2024 by A'Besa Hodge

All rights reserved.

No part of this book may be reproduced or transmitted in any form or by any means, electronic or mechanical, including photocopying, recording, or by any information storage and retrieval system, without permission in writing from the copyright author, except for the use of brief quotations in a book review.

ISBN: 978-1-63960-035-9 Paperback
      978-1-63960-036-6 Ebook

Published in the United States by
Pen2Pad Ink Publishing www.penpadink.org.

Requests to publish work from this book or to contact the author should be sent to: abesahodge@yahoo.com

Groupings at the end of the book are from Hammond, Frank, and Ida Mae Hammond. Pigs In The Parlor. Impact Christian Books, 2008. pp. 128-129.

Gloriasteen Dennis

This book is dedicated to my beautiful mother, Gloriasteen Dennis who taught me how to pray and intercede when times were good and bad. My mother prayed for me, supported me and encouraged me to have Faith in God no matter what.
(Fly High Mama)

Intro

My mother's timeless wisdom always echoes in my heart: "Make sure you have some prayers stored up because you never know when you're going to have to go back to them." This resonates profoundly, reminding us that adversity can strike when we least expect it, testing our faith and resilience.

This book is for anyone who feels like they don't have a prayer life, or they don't know what and how to pray, when my mother passed away September 20th, 2022 I felt like I was disconnected from God because of the pain that paralyzed me from my mother's death, so I began to pray to God (remembering what my mom taught me) asking him to turn my Pain into Purpose, so God turned my Words into prayers and I began confessing and praying these words on a daily basis and I believe God heard my cry and received my prayers.

Acknowledging and Appreciating God

Here's a few ways I acknowledge God when I wake up at 4AM:

Lord,

I want to thank You for another day that wasn't promised to me, giving me another chance to make it right with You.

Lord,

I thank You for being the one and only true living God.

Lord,

I thank You that You loved me so much that You gave Your only begotten Son.

Lord,

Thank You for laying me and my family down last night and waking us up this morning. In Jesus' Name.

Lord,

Thank You for Your Grace and Mercy.

Lord,

Thank You for loving me unconditionally; thank You for not killing me. I realize I've sinned against You and You only.

4 Things You Need When You Pray:

1. Faith

2. Consistency

3. Always end your prayer In Jesus' Name

4. Be intentional about praying

Lord,

Please give me the wisdom, energy, and patience to do what You called me to do. In Jesus' Name.

Lord,

Please let the words of my mouth and the meditation of my heart be acceptable in Your sight. In Jesus' Name.

Psalms 19:14 NIV

Lord,

Please show me what You need me to see today and please give me the courage to receive what You show me. In Jesus' Name.

Lord,

Please deliver me from my secret struggles (*call out your struggles*). You can't get delivered if you refuse to acknowledge your struggles.

Lord,

Please create in me a clean heart and renew a right spirit within me. In Jesus' Name.

Psalms 51:10 KJV

Lord,

Please let this mind be in me that is also in Christ Jesus. In Jesus' Name.

Philippians 2:5 KJV

Lord,

Please give me the faith to trust You in everything I do. In Jesus' Name.

Lord,

Please forgive me for my sins. The ones I know of and the ones I don't know of. In Jesus' Name.

(Don't hesitate to call out the sins you know of)

Lord,

Please protect me and my family from all hurt, harm and danger. In Jesus' Name.

Lord,

Please give me and my family traveling grace, and please protect us from road rage, gun violence.

Lord,

Please cleanse
my heart, my
mind and my body
from all toxicity
and negativity.
In Jesus' Name.

Lord,

Bless me to be the answer to somebody's prayer.
In Jesus' Name.

Lord,

Please keep me even when I don't want to be kept
In Jesus' Name.

Lord,

Please forgive me for the lust of the eye, the lust of the flesh, and the pride of life. In Jesus' Name.

Lord,

Please, please heal my heart from the people and things that hurt me. In Jesus' Name.

Lord,

Please give me the strength to make it through this day, week, month, year.
In Jesus' Name.

Lord,

Please deliver me from bitterness and unforgiveness. In Jesus' Name.

Lord,

Please bless and cover my home, my community, my city, my state, and the world.
In Jesus' Name.

Lord,

Please deliver
me from my
addictions
(call them out)
In Jesus Name.

*Only you and
God know your
real additions.*

Lord,

Please bless me not to think myself to be higher or better than anyone else.

Lord,

Please remove all fear an replace it with faith. In Jesus' Name.

Lord,

Please remove all depression, anxiety, worry and suicidal thoughts from my heart and mind. In Jesus' Name.

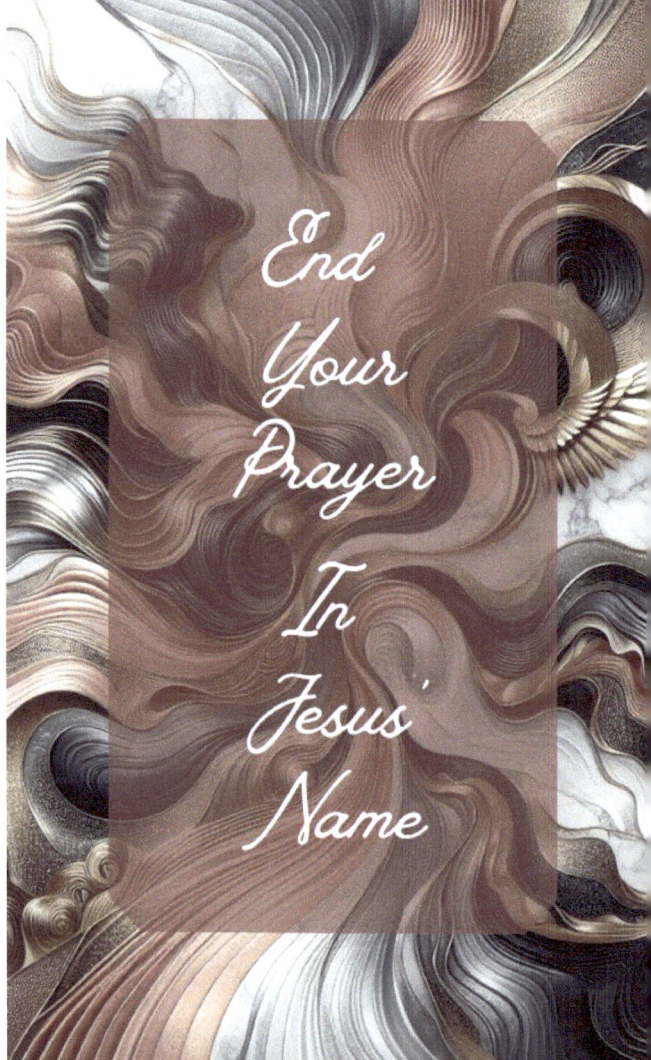

Lord,

Before You change my situation, please change my spirit. In Jesus' Name.

Lord,

Please don't let my loyalty turn into slavery.
In Jesus' Name.

(Sometimes we can be too loyal).

Lord,

Please bless me to always seek You first before making any decisions. In Jesus' Name.

 Lord,

Please remove any curses that have been spoken against me and my family.

Ask God to remove the curses:
Off your finances
Off your marriage
Off your children

Lord,

Please bless me to be a good example and not a poor excuse. In Jesus' Name.

Lord,

Please bless me to stop creating problems in my head that doesn't exist. In Jesus' Name.

(Most of the time we overthink)

Lord,

Please bless my friends, my so-called friends, and enemies *(call them out)*. In Jesus' Name.

Lord,

Please deliver me from childhood and adult trauma, abandonment, and rejection. In Jesus' Name.

Lord,

Bless me to think the right thoughts and say the right words in every situation I face. In Jesus' Name.

Lord,

Please protect me and my family from any chaos/confusion that comes our way. In Jesus' Name.

Lord,

Please deliver me from the people and things that are draining me. In Jesus Name.

(Most of the time you know who and what they are.)

Lord,

Please remove all laziness and procrastination from my mind and body today. In Jesus' Name.

(Sometimes we get stuck)

Lord,

Bless me to learn how to show up for myself before showing up for others. In Jesus' Name.

Lord,

Before I try to forgive somebody else, please bless me to forgive myself. In Jesus' Name.

Lord,

Please remove every distraction in my life that's assigned to destroy my dreams. In Jesus' Name.

Lord,

Please bring peace to my confusion, joy to my sadness, and hope to my heart. In Jesus' Name.

Lord,

Please bless me not to cut off the people who you've ordained to be a blessing to me, In Jesus' Name.

Lord,

If it's not for me, then please remove it, and if they're not for me, please reveal it. In Jesus' Name.

Lord,

I pray for a divine *healing* here on Earth *(call out everything that you need God to heal in your body). Please mend everything that's* broken *and make me whole. In Jesus' Name.*

Lord,

Please protect me both emotionally and mentally to deal with toxic people and a toxic environment. In Jesus' Name.

Addiction Prayer:

Lord,

Please take the thought out of my head, the smell out of my nose, the taste out of my mouth and the desire out of my heart, In Jesus' Name.

Lord,

Please bless my wife (call out her name). Build her up where she is torn down and give her the strength to submit herself unto me as unto The Lord.
In Jesus' Name.

Ephesians 5:23

Lord,

Please bless my husband *(call out his name)*. Build him up where he is torn down and strengthen him to love me the way that Christ loved The Church.

Lord,

Please bless my children and grandchildren to have a good day. Bless them not to be picked out to be picked on, bless them not to be bullied and please bless them not to be a bully.
In Jesus' Name.

Lord,

Please bless (child's name) to do the right thing and make the right decisions today. Lord, bless them not to get caught up in anything that can destroy or damage their lives or careers. Lord, please cover them and protect them from all hurt, harm, and danger.
Lord, please grant favor over their lives.
In Jesus' Name.

Lord,

I pray for every school, college, and university. Lord, please protect every person on every campus that I'm connected with *(call out schools, colleges, universities)* In Jesus' Name.

Lord,

Please take my pain and turn it into purpose. In Jesus' Name.

(The prayer I prayed after I lost my mom)

Lord,

Please convict me, and show me myself when I'm not doing the things that You called me to do. In Jesus' Name.

Lord,

Please make *it* stop!
In Jesus Name

(State whatever
is *torturing*
or *tormenting* you.)

Lord,

Please help me!
In Jesus Name

(Sometimes that's all you can say.)

Salvation Prayer:

Dear Lord,

I come to You asking for you to forgive me for all of my sins In the name of Jesus. Your Word says, "Whosoever shall call on the name of the Lord shall be saved" (Acts 2:21).

Today I am calling on you, asking for you to come into my heart and be Lord over my life according to Romans 10:9-10. In Jesus name.

These groupings are just a suggestion of what might be encountered. This is just to offer some insight into the problems caused by spirits. I was able to call out some of the things that I was struggling with by looking at these groupings:

Hammond, Frank, and Ida Mae Hammond. Pigs In The Parlor. Impact Christian Books, 2008. pp. 128-129.

Bitterness:

Unforgiveness
Anger
Retaliation
Hatred
Resentment
Violence
Bad Temper
Accusation
Judging
Criticism
Fault Finding

Persecution:

Fear of Condemnation

Fear of Judgement

Unfairness

Fear of Accusation

Perfection:	**Addiction:**
Criticism	Alcohol
Ego	Drugs
Vanity	Nicotine
Pride	Medication
Anger	Caffeine
Intolerance	

Depression:	**Covetousness:**
Discouragement	Greed
Hopelessness	Stealing
Suicide	Jealousy
Despair	Discontent

Pride:

Arrogance
Ego
Vanity
Self-Righteousness
Importance

Indecision:

Compromise
Confusion
Procrastination
Forgetfulness

Insecurity:

Self-Pity
Loneliness
Timidity
Inferiority

Worry:

Fear
Anxiety
Dread

Insecurity:

Self-Pity
Loneliness
Timidity
Inferiority

Jealousy:

Selfishness
Envy
Distrust

Guilt:

Embarrassment
Shame
Condemnation
Unworthiness

www.ingramcontent.com/pod-product-compliance
Lightning Source LLC
Chambersburg PA
CBHW041722070526
44585CB00001B/12